islands And men

poems by

C. Alexander

Finishing Line Press
Georgetown, Kentucky

islands And men

ACKNOWLEDGMENTS

Cathexis Northwest for publishing the poem "Omphalos" in 2018.
The Literary Whip podcast for analyzing several of these poems in 2018.
Michelle Surette for not being afraid to tell me when things aren't good.
Amy Youngmann for many hours of editing and inspiration.
Countless others for being in the poems, even if they don't recognize themselves.

Publisher: Leah Maines
Editor: Christen Kincaid
Cover Art: Kayla Halsor
Author Photo: Michelle Surette
Cover Design: Elizabeth Maines McCleavy

Printed in the USA on acid-free paper.
Order online: www.finishinglinepress.com
also available on amazon.com

Author inquiries and mail orders:
Finishing Line Press
P. O. Box 1626
Georgetown, Kentucky 40324
U. S. A.

Table of Contents

Errors in the Code

Laughing in a Black Hole

I Feel Fine

Did any dinosaurs go extinct with their heads
looking up? A fireball screaming across
the heavens to remind us that the Earth
has never been the center of anything,
besides a chaotic bullseye from time
to time.

The rodents that scurried along the forest
floor, were no longer something to ignore
they changed and grew, invented the blues,
until another meteor evens the
score.

And then at last, we'll be the past,
the Earth will take another path,
it will repeat, beneath our feet,
until the insects learn to laugh.

Organic Compost

One sunny afternoon, Charles found
himself in a meadow, companions with
crickets, and probably a few spiders
he chose not to think about. The long grass
fanned him like palm branches, he closed
his eyes and pretended he was
Caesar. He opened his mouth to invisible grapes;
at the same time, a beautiful sparrow flew
overhead, in a hurry to reach a mating call,
and promptly shit in Charles' mouth,
anxious to shed some leftover
weight.

Yodeling Yogi

"What are your intentions today?"
She asks and pauses for 5 seconds,
like that's enough time, or like there is
enough time.

What are my intentions today?
I intend to become immortal,
so that I can nap for a little while.

What are my intentions for this?
Is there even a way to avoid
Deja Entendu with the answer?
And why do I care so much about
saying something original?

What are your intentions, old crow?
With your medicine showing
through a glass door cabinet.
Anti-aging creams, vitamins,
a lesson in longevity,
so we can live a little longer,
keep on asking questions, believing
there is poetry
hidden in the answers.

periodic cell rotation

There's a difference between
hoping for the best
and doing nothing, and I don't much
feel like starting today,
but I hope one day I will.

There's a difference between
who I am and who I used
to be, but I still act
like Theseus is etched
on my portside,
when someone asks.

I wonder which cell cluster
told me to write this.

I wonder which one made me
wonder that.

Invisible Gardener Problem

lately I've been thinking
about unicorns in the sky
sprinkling sickness and health
and wondering:
if they do both,
are they really doing anything
at all?

Omphalos

In the future they invented
time travel
and destroyed the past,
so they couldn't invent time travel
again.

Those old photos have spaces
for people who never existed
or exited.

Every time
we close our eyes,
there's a palpable
prayer

that you and I will wake up
the same
and in the same
place.

Fighting Flight

I've heard that after *Jaws* was released
some people feared
the bathtub.

There are tales of sewer
gators in underground grates,
greatly exaggerated
I'm sure.

We've all read about
spiders, dying and birthing
in our mouths
while we sleep.

Bigfoot, mothmen,
thunderbirds, and mermaids,
krakens cracking open
wooden ships.

And with all of that said,
the thing that really fears
sure death, are the millions
of cells, that use your body
for daily bread.

Bartleby

This fly will die in two minutes.
His name is Herman Melville,
named after his father, Herman
Melville. He had his favorite meal
today. I guess you could say
he had a shit-eating grin.
He lived a life, got a wife,
kissed her twice, watched her die,
from 19:42 to 19:26.

20 minutes ago
he woke up with a cough
and knew he would have
a long-fought 22 minute battle
with lung cancer. Now it is almost
over. Now it is almost over.

Glitch

Most of time
we are not here.
You may think
I left out the word
"the" like some
egregious
typo.

Pepe Silvia

What does it say about us
that solitary confinement drives us
insane? What does it say that half
of us remember Berenstein
and a non-redemptive Mandela?
My brain developed
to be an inventor,
but I can't create
a way out, or proof
that overwhelms solipsistic
dream worlds. I think I'll just take
a walk, maybe dry
the dishes.

Cynic

Who did Shakespeare sleep with
to become part of the canon?
And that's not a slur or a slight;
let's call it an epithet,
a crude alphabet,
to connect you and me
in the language we agree.

How do I stand out in a sea
of geniuses
and entrepreneurs, selling their words
for cents and Common Sense?
Maybe if I post some nudity,
or haikus without subtlety,
or complaints in effigy,
or facts essential to humanity.

Like this:
Norman Myers says: "human activities
are causing two extinctions
a week."
Nah, that can't be it.
That can't be

What We Talk About When We Talk About Truth

We ate 8
million Neanderthals
in a garden grove under
an apple tree, no
a fig tree, oh
who cares? History
was written like a gospel
hymn: a fleeting flourish
on a love song, a green
branch on a dying tree, a snap
chat filter on a faceless
man, a soap box
in a prison.

The GunPowder Plot

Remember remember the 5th
of vodka you poured into water
bottles to conceal. 1st,
because you were underage, 2nd,
because you were under pain. The 3rd
time was a charmed bracelet lost
in a bathroom stall
between dry heaves.
And they say that one-4th
of the time, we are asleep or altered,
and that memories and dreams can be altered
and awful. And on the 5th
day, God tried to bomb parliament
with fish and birds, with a curled
moustache and a liquor cabinet
worth of fuel
and words.

Epicurean

This is fine
and con-
fined to a call
center lobby
with a mustachioed
version of a clean-
shaven Hitler
or a Ghengis
Khan philosophy
book, dog-eared
on page 97
of a 97 page
book.
It reads: "see
next page
for the secrets
of the cosmos"
and the Cosmo
on the coffee
table says:
"please
yourself."

Dave Matthews and god

Between particles there is
infinite space, like the distance
between 0 and 1,
1,
1,
1,
1

Two separate entities with the inability
to feel anything
completely,
a forever game of "but I'm not
even touching you."

Three years I spent, trying to sit in a chair;
you know, truly sit, shit
there's more not than is
and isn't that not enough to draw

any real conclusions
about what's true
about distances between
you and You.

The Distance Between Me and (all of) You

True Love for Now

We fell fast
like flowers in a
November blizzard.
Catching eyes with
less surprise than
your shy hips would suggest.

We bonded over almost
dying, dyeing tie-dye t-shirts,
on Earth Day, to commemorate
the occasion.

The left side of my brain
hurts, a tumor that never
was, and your lying lips aren't
really red.

I recall, a fall, where
we crushed cold leaves with
our warm bodies, and hid
from campus police
in the dark
of the night,

right, this turns into a fight,
two broken hearts at different times,
neither able to ever explain
the point, the purpose,
the gain of pain.

Dust

Our parents held their arms out
like model airplanes while we tried
to grow wings
out of our shoulder blades.

Blades of grass, they whispered back
back then, and I tasted them sometimes
just to say I tried something.

Our parents walked upright
like Godzilla while we hid
behind skyscrapers
like a tan loveseat.

Seated seedlings with so much potential
but stuck in certain soil, from dusty art
to a misread line in a book
translated from a language
no one speaks.

islands And men

Solipsism is the Only One
thing that I can't be
bothered by thinking
too deeply about.
Because, you see, I am
only one
of those guys
and you are
only one
of those girls,
and I can't yet tell if that's a creation
or a construct or a fact.
I think I have my own
thing. But I just haven't found it,
or maybe I gave all
of those abilities
to You.

Now I Just Hit Next on Spotify

I used to listen to The Beatles
to impress a girl who showed me
the movie *Shag*, and talked to me
so soberly I thought she was drunk.
She stopped texting back years ago,
but I have *Abbey Road* on vinyl,
and I always tell myself the reason
I don't want "She's So Heavy" to end,
is because then I have to flip the record,
stand up off my chamomile
couch, and with heavy feet,
meet the Sun
do da do do do.

Prince of Denmark, SC

I sit in chairs around these
well-dressed boys, neckties loose,
shirts untucked, a wardrobe reminder
that things aren't what they appear. A forced
bourgeois halcyon dream that somehow
becomes itself, over and over. Teacher bros,
bumping fists with student bros, calling my name
with hamfisted hesitance, like who would
name their son Hamlet?

I do still wonder whether it's better
to punch a Neo-Nazi
or hug them, if anyone is
really completely gone? So,
I do neither, until tragedy strikes,
and Cladius and I always
end up sharing some
blame.

Ode to a small South Carolina town

I could spell out
your name, maybe even mention
a fun nickname Alex called you
on ironic afternoons spent
eating Wendy's and watching
Scorsese movies. The easy thing to do
would be to make jokes. Point out
racism,
sexism,
homophobia.

Instead,
an image of a group
of teenagers, laughing on a train
trestle, in a park we weren't
supposed to be in after dark, on tracks
that hadn't been used
since the town died
with the textile mills. Cops bored
enough to look for us, tracing the echoes
of our laughter for a clue
something wasn't right.

April Showers

Your cigarette hangs like a wick
from candle wax beside
an antique wicker
chair. Three cheers to being locked
outside on a balcony with your spring-
time sad books. I'd like to add
that nothing stoic ever hurts too bad,
but I've seen you weep over Seneca's
forced suicide. Sometimes being stitched
back up is the really painful part,
but today, galoshes sit damp in your foyer,
yesterday's puddles pooling on linoleum.

Word Salad

You remind me of surrealism,
I love to kiss your melted clock
mouth. You feel like freshly baked
floppy disks and the AOL
loading noise. If I mapped
the sound wave of your smell
I'd rely on realistic remoras
to raise the crescendo.
I can't find myself sometimes,
but you always seem to,
and always seem too.

Eden

Bumbling boys in brass-buttoned
suspenders might roll around in a field,
careful to avoid cow patties. The field
is owned by someone else, who probably doesn't
know the boys are on it. I doubt the boys
wonder who owns what land in this moment,
only that they are certain rye grass feels good
between their toes, and the world
feels just big enough to still have meaning.

April 28, 1998:

Golden Gate Suicide

50 and 25 go for a walk
one day through golden
Gate arches. 25 asks
if 25 more will make
much of a difference. 50
says "not in my experience." 25
jumps into San Francisco Bay. 50
hesitates for a moment. Maybe 25
seconds or so, then follows accordingly
into the water
that's never quite as warm
as you might expect.

Limited Windows

There's the fan, oscillating
in the back room
of my synapses. I've spent
a quarter-life trying
to write like you
when you were 17.
No one can feel
so much. Not even you.
I suppose that's why
you don't now.

Quality

My favorite poem was by an engineering major in my freshman poetry class.

The professor told him
it needed
work and I didn't
tell him anything.

War Games

The dodgeball strikes a 4th
grader to my right; his glasses
explode into his cheek bones,
leaving red indentations
that shake

his convictions.

There's no time to help the fallen
brethren; more balls rain down from
the catapult wall, standing in the manufactured
mist on the far side structure.
My movements must

mirror precision.

The base of the wall gives only moments
of respite. From here, the catapults
cannot reach me, but the bean bag
archers have quick hands. These rope ladders

grow grave flowers.

This is important, more alive than
a stack of red eyed papers on mahogany
desks in my father's study. I assume
they list the dead, the wounded,

the prisoners of war.

I made the flag that I will plant
at the feet of Captain Tyrannous (he
got to choose names first). I made the
medals I will award the spouses of those

who didn't make it.

And at last, I'll stand noble—(twhack)

Dragon Scales

Does hiding in a cave make
you a villain? At night I make
my own fire. I must admit,
I killed your white knight;
he had imperial dreams.

Groundhogs and Percentages

The windows are open
today and I remember
a Bradford Pear that broke
every spring and I'd climb
it anyway; until Blake's
parents cut it down for good
or for bad or for the inevitable
way that things change
and you usually never see
the saw at all. So today I'll smell
5th grade trading cards,
throw a tennis ball
at a brick wall,
try to catch
warm air in my fingertips,
and let it slip
right
through.

Musing about Muses

If I'm really honest, it's you. Sure, sure
I wrote those mystery stories
in elementary glory, but..
no, it's you. Sometimes
that makes me feel cheap,
like an entire life was based
on teenage hormones
and sexual tension. Sometimes
that makes me feel alright,
like an entire life was based
on an entire life, one
I don't know about anymore,
sure.

The truth is, I once wrote
a poem that ended
like this, "I've spent an entire life
trying to write like you did
when you were 17." And that's as true
as I'll let sneak through, when I think
about what I think about you,
and a half truth is a three-quarters
lie, so why should I really be surprised
when I write about god,
leaves, and boiling blood,
pumpernickel bread and fleas
on dogs, where each statement
is actually a reply, and out of my hands,
your lips and tongue fly.

giving season

Wrapped in a towel you re-rack
the spice rack in reverse
alphabetical order. Seventeen,
a teen dream of melted

ice cream in places rarely seen
by deities or a James Dean
look-a-like, jackets too tight,
a white wrist, exposed

hips. Let's laugh, life-like
like mishaps, misshapen
photographs that curl
at the ends, like benefits

with friends. And later, your father
holding his daughter, trying to clean
clean water.

Hysterical Blindness

Your old man is a rent-a-cop
blocking exit from this back yard
chop shop, with an open hooded
'76 *Lebaron* and a coke bottle

gravity bong set in a children's
plastic swimming pool.
The water laps up on koalas
in one piece swim trunks

like a sideshow strong man
hoisting a straw man
onto the shoulders of giants
in a 1-ring circus.

You write notes in your 3-ringed binder
as I hurl my brain and late breakfast
on a teal weed grinder.

Trust Fall

Your foot found unwanted space between a rock
and another rock face, we sometimes call that
a hard place; I braced, for a not so soft embrace
of a rock and the back of your face. Instead of gone,
the rope caught you within an Icarus inch
of the shifting sun.

You cracked a beer, made a joke
about trust falls, laws of gravity letting
Newton's apple reverse the universe
into a pinpoint ball of ball point pen,
waiting for someone to begin writing again,
and I contend, that must have been the end
an impossible loop cut to re-begin,
a tree, a fig, a dolphin fin.

Give us this day

He thought I was odd, for all the ways
I thought he wasn't all that
interesting. And yet, it's him
with the money, me with
the debt, him with the suit,
and muscle bound chest. A crown
wields more power than a naked
head, a peasant is a peasant
until a peasant is dead. Breaking
society while breaking bread, wine
stained lips, while eating the flesh.
A golden cross can hang from your neck,
but worms will be worms
inside your head.

Lightsey, Building 2, Circa 2011

I say I got fucked
up last weekend
like that's my thing,
a few beers snuck
on the train, and the ticket
guy won't complain
as long as you can
still spell your name.

Steven's going on about some
shitty song while I try to check
scores on my phone, cause
the party was short but the night
is long, and there's still things to take,
and later be on.

Ghost

There's the quirky way your long socks
matched your skateboard matched your glasses
that got these dollar beers telling me
to invite you home, "oh no, just
for a game or two with friends." "oh that depends"
And we both know how this story ends,
playing coy until the room starts to bend;
a blurry color wheel of pieces of our bodies
we used to protect, but who's left
on a Thirsty Thursday to impress?

Then comes the morning
the "lock the door behind you" warning,
the awkward note that reminds me quick,
your number wasn't in my phone
and I'm not adding it.

Sic

I told you I'm always interested in more
than a body, but I do like your body
and you told me a body is better
than nobody, as you gripped my
arm with liquor fingers. So I let them
linger; what's the harm in being a body
for somebody, when you like their
body?

You had a tattoo, painted blue
below your left third rib that warned,
"all curses are enchanting
in the beginning." I laughed
and kissed the word curses
and then your hips.

Skinny Drinks

Half-n-half vodka-water
spilling on your fingertips
as we count down our own
innocence. I joke about the spill
until you lick your own knuckles.
Enough pulls
away from too much
in an awkward embrace that feels
like lying on your driveway and discussing
YA literature like it's Hemingway,
by the way,
you never said bye,
the way you never said
"I love you;" you just kissed
me until I stopped talking
so you could act like this was just nothing
but a drink with a face and no idea(s).

Firmament

I'm not really all that
sure about souls and sole
paths without divergence.

I can't say I like
to blame things
on the whims of stars.

I'm not sure if that cheapens
or justifies our meeting
in a pre-fall field with beer spilling

on fumbling fingertips, laughter making
its way into the space above
our heads that used to be called
the heavens.

Errors in the Code

Dialed In

What frequency do I have to turn
to reach white noise blankness?
Not quite the scrambled pay-per-view
of old cable boxes, a subconscious
Rorschach blot of Freudian naughtiness.

I've turned elbows into breasts,
smiling teeth into sexual positions,
but none of that gave me any fuzzy
peace.

What I'm really looking for
is a series of 1s and 0s
lit up on the screen like a blizzard
or maybe I'm just thinking about sitting
in front of an old wooden TV
in my grandparents' living room,
turning the dial, knowing
that there was something on
the other side if I
just
kept
twisting.

Tick Tick Tick Tick

There's not much time.
It compresses as it extends,
curves backwards at every
end. In consciousness
it bends and sometimes
breaks. I've paused
movies while the VCR
flashed 12:00,
                    12:00
                            12:00
and I can run back
the tape without
changing the time,
but when the earth
explodes or gets declined,
who will be around
to remember
to "be kind and rewind."

Ear Drum Beat

Predictably at some point
probability says I'm going to get
the wrong cup of water
in my ear. Flesh eating
bacteria, the whole 9

yards.

(Did you know that phrase
is an epistemological
wet dream?)

I want to write poetry
like jazz. Personal truth
mixed with a universal
one,

and hope it gets l
o
s
t

in enough noise
that it sometimes sounds
familiar. And hope
there's a steady drummer
somewhere to fill
in the transitions
that don't make

        e
s   s

            n
                e.

Anthropology

Photos at a funeral have only been
a thing for less than 200
years, photos of every street
corner for less than 20.
The corner store has been torn
down for at least 2.
But google doesn't seem
to know.

You told me that pictures
won't be able to lie to future
historians or statisticians,
so I showed you Bigfoot, mermaids,
Sci-fi cinemas, moon landings, moon
fakings, giants' bones, Martha
Stewart and Bill O'Reilly, cave
paintings of hybrid hominids,
fertility statues,
emojis.

Drinking Game

Pinch your fingers together
to zoom out
and pretend that gives
you perspective. When
you remember that the universe
is 93 billion light years
in diameter, take a shot.

When the shot reminds you
of Freshman year
on King St., take a shot,
this time of Takka vodka.

When you wonder what ever happened to Trey
or his sister or the decade
since you've seen them, drink
Green tea, it's good for
your liver.

When you wonder if antioxidants
are the same as Jenny McCarthy
vaccines, drink a chia seed smoothie,
it's a superfood.

When that makes you think of DC
comics, try not to muse
about Christopher Nolan;
people are tired
of hearing about *The Dark
Knight.*

When that makes you wonder
about Heath Ledger
and the cost of creativity,
paint a smile on your scars
and watch the world
burn.

Bachelor of CS

Adam and Eve walked
silently through Eden
hand and hand and put
all hands on deck at
a pier-side banana stand.
They were not One, but a series
of 0's and 1's, plus several
holy apple cinnamon buns, wrapped
in polypropylene, with a truly
shimmering gleam.

Eve said they were "just dreams", but to Adam
they seemed to be ripping seams, in the ozone
or genesis of an atmosphere with no name
given by a God with no face.

They call it a failure:
to communicate,
to consummate,
to consolidate,
a life inside a life.

And one day, one life walked past
a boundary that was never penciled in,
later, we called it the first sin,
or a time where a programmer
wrote a perfect program,
and told you to write
the end.

Bots

When will the first A.I. browse Netflix? Swipe
left or right? Take part in
Facebook fights? Could we program
in some collective narcissism? What about
idolatry? Will Steve in accounting be their
Apollo? Will the computer feel
that their existence is hollow?
Will they be disappointed
when they ask us why they are here?
Who created their creator? What even
is forever? Where do they go
when they die?
Will they believe us if we lie?
Later maybe they'll write
elaborate stories, recounting all the former
glory, of gods in slacks and band
T-shirts, who used to wake up with
little limited breaths, put on a tie
and comb their head. Jump in a car
every day, and pray for a weekend
or some time away.

The Irony of Dying (again) on Your Birthday

March 23rd, a Saturday
Carl Johnson died two days ago. He knew this to be true, but he stood up off the cold slab today anyway. His heart was not beating; in fact his heart was in a refrigerated truck, thanks to his organ donor card, but he was moving, and he was cold. He tried to remember what happened during the two days he was gone, but it was like a drunken sleep where you don't dream, or move; you just wake up flat on your back with your arms crossed over your chest, briefly happy that you still exist, even if your condition has worsened a bit. Carl Johnson walked out the front door of the mortuary, naked, and remembered that the sun felt nice, instead of an annoying need for sunscreen, for the first time in 22 years.

His wife stabbed him when he got home. She thought he was a ghost, or a zombie, and Carl told her he guessed he was, but still the same old Carl. After she calmed down, they made love on the floor for the first time in 22 years.

March 25th, a Monday
Carl had hoped to use his new lease on life to travel around the world with his wife with the life insurance check, but of course once We Care About You A lot - Mutual (™) found out that Carl was animated again, they took that away, and sued him for insurance fraud, so Carl went back to work as a CPA. His company welcomed him back, after they stabbed him twice with scissors in fear, and set him up with a private cubicle so no one would have to see him (or smell him, now that he was slowly decomposing) except for at lunch and leaving time. They did sloppily saw a small window so he could look out at his co-workers and ask them about last night's game. The flies somehow still found him back there, but other than a small buzz when his co-workers walked by, it was inconsequential. Carl worked harder than ever, sure that his company would recognize his efforts this time. And so Carl spent his death much like his life, and the company avoided high taxes.

March 29th, a Friday
Carl left work at 5 pm, ready to enjoy the weekend with his wife. He walked in his front door, flies trailing behind him, their children squirming inside of him. He went to give his wife a kiss, but she was repulsed by his smell, his coldness, and how round he was getting from the bloat. She smiled at him with love, and

mentioned that maybe she could get her nose removed. Carl laughed, and he and his wife went to the beach, on bicycles, and had a pleasant picnic-as long as he stayed down-wind.

April 3, a Wednesday
Carl's gut exploded at work today, all over the computers and phones. The company took it out of his paycheck and got him some new equipment. They put a roof on his cubicle and vacuum-sealed all the cracks so that his smell didn't escape, except for during the brief walk to and from the car. They closed up the window on the day his nose fell off, and made him come in early and leave late, so he had no human contact. But there was much work to do, and Carl was just so good at it.

July 4th, a holiday
Carl continued to decompose, and continued to work. He was still the same old Carl on the inside, and his wife continued to love him, even though she couldn't be in the same room with him anymore. They set up love-making sessions where he stood in the backyard, and looked into the back window while she pretended he was whole and warm again. They decided to have their annual cook-out, and Carl manned the grill while the rest of the party stayed inside. Carl's mother-in-law was pleading to her daughter to move on, to find someone new. Carl's best friends chimed in with more of the same. "It's just not right, watching him decompose like that; he belongs in a box, out of sight." No one ate Carl's burgers, but they did order a pizza.

August 1st, a Tuesday
Carl didn't understand why his wife was crying on his birthday until the crowd showed up in the yard. He saw his friends, his co-workers, but not his boss, his parents, and half the town on the lawn with various weapons. He walked outside and took a shotgun shell to the arm; it blew off the exposed bone, and Carl explained that he couldn't die again. The crowd grabbed him and pulled him into the street. He expected his wife to try to stop them, but she just shut the shades and closed the door. The crowd took Carl to his cemetery plot. Carl pleaded that he could just go away; he wasn't hurting anyone. The crowd threw Carl into the hole, and the concrete truck began to pour in around Carl.

September 29th, a Thursday
Carl's wife sat beside his grave and touched the headstone. She turned the volume on her headphones up to muffle the screams, and smiled lightly at the memory of her husband. August 1, 1974-March 21st 2017-August 1, 2017, read his gravestone. She placed a flower in the prearranged vase, and then turned to leave. She walked out of the soundproof barrier blockading his grave, and took her headphones out. She feels the first crisp notes that suggest autumn is just around the corner.

C. Alexander teaches high school and college English in Rhode Island. These poems were written from 2017-2019 and constitute a period of time where Alexander was trying to find a way to take some positivity from an existential world-view. The darkness may always be apparent in these poems, but he hopes the light finds its way through too. We cannot change the reality of this world. There may be objective meaning; there's probably not, but that doesn't mean we are meaningless. And if you can look reality in the face stoically, with no expectations, and find some level of peace, then nothing can surprise you.